Five Moving Average Signals That
Back Tested Stock Marke

By Steve Burns & Holly Burns

5 MOVING AVERAGE SIGNALS THAT BEAT BUY AND HOLD

BACK TESTED STOCK MARKET SIGNALS

STEVE BURNS
HOLLY BURNS

Disclaimer

This book is meant to be informational and shouldn't be used as trading or investing advice. All readers should gather information from multiple sources to create their personalized investment strategies and trading systems. The authors make no guarantees related to the claims contained herein. Always seek the advice of a competent licensed professional before implementing any plan or system that involves your money. Please invest and trade responsibly.

FOREWORD

"There are only two things you can really do when a new bear market begins: sell and get out or go short. When you get out, you should stay out until the bear market is over." - William J. O'Neil

---

This book was written for traders and investors that are frustrated with their stock market returns, and for readers who were fans of buy and hold until they witnessed (or felt) the crash of 1987, the NASDAQ bubble of 2000, or the 2008-2009 financial meltdown. It's also for traders interested in the basics of trend following and quantified trading signals. This book won't tell you how to make easy money or get rich quick. It presents an alternative to buy and hold investing, including examples of potential entry and exit signals based on the current price action rather than market timing. Market timing fails because it tries to be predictive about an unpredictable future.

This book will demonstrate systematic ways to know when to be in, and when to go to cash before the next bear market, crash, or financial panic. The goal is to be in during bull markets and out before bear markets. The systems described within are on the same time frame as buy and hold investors, and are meant to be compared to buy and hold for long-term returns and maximum drawdowns, not against other investing or trading systems.

All trading systems have specific goals for returns and drawdowns in capital. The goal of this book is to beat buy and hold investing in returns and drawdowns with less emotional pain and financial stress.

The systems described in this book are long side only because the short side is difficult to trade with a passive approach. To sell short in this way is to fight against the long-term trend of the entire market. The easiest money is on the long side of the stock indexes. We have omitted the short side because it is rarely worth the risk.

This book introduces the concept of reactive signal based technical analysis used by trend following traders, but it is only one way to make money, there are many others. I hope this book will give you something to think about when you are deciding how to invest your money, and if you do decide to try these strategies for yourself, that it will show you how trend following traders get on the right side of a long-term trend and stay there for as long as possible.

ONE

CAN YOU BEAT BUY AND HOLD?

"In financial economics, the efficient-market hypothesis (EMH) states that asset prices fully reflect all available information. A direct implication is that it is impossible to "beat the market" consistently on a risk-adjusted basis since market prices should only react to new information or changes in discount rates (the latter may be predictable or unpredictable)." - Wikipedia

---

In Many Trading and investment circles, it is assumed that the markets can't be beaten by investors or traders for a long period. It is accepted that all investment methodologies and trading systems revert to even at some point. It is common practice for many investors to buy a basket of diversified stocks and hold them, forever. But who does this philosophy benefit? Mutual fund companies, personal finance planners, and Wall Street.

If it isn't impossible to beat buy and hold, then how do we explain the traders and investors featured in Jack Schwager's "Market

Wizard" series and Michael Covel's "Trend Followers"? Or the long-term success of investors like Warren Buffet or George Soros? Were they all just lucky, or did they apply an edge to investing and trading? Just because some people can't beat the market consistently doesn't mean no one can. Just because 99.9% of the population can't play professional sports doesn't mean it's impossible. The managed mutual fund industry is the bastion of buy and hold investing, but it the best strategy?

Per the New York Times, of the 2862 U.S. stock mutual funds that existed in March 2009, not one has beaten the market. They weren't positioned correctly to benefit from the rebound after the financial panic of 2008. How many mutual funds routinely beat the market year after year? Zero.

When you buy a managed mutual fund, the odds are that the manager will not be the next Peter Lynch, but instead someone who will charge you a management fee for underperforming their bench-mark index. Mutual fund management fees will decrease your invest-ment capital over the long-term, chipping away at your money little by little and year after year. You could lose 1% to 2% of your capital to fees each year and limit your ability to grow your capital. Mutual fund managers have a good business model that serves them well. You, as the investor, take all the risk while they get paid set fees regardless of their performance.

Mutual fund managers collect big fees for the expectation of doing one thing: beating their benchmark. Managers of mutual funds that invest in big cap stocks should, at a minimum, beat the S&P 500 index exchange traded fund SPY to justify their fees. If they can't do that, what's their purpose? Over the long-term, 80% of mutual funds don't beat their benchmarks. The truth is that the SPY ETF beats 80% of active managed mutual funds, most of the time.

The SPY ETF beats 80% of mutual fund managers for five primary reasons:

- The SPY ETF has a small management fee of .09%.

- Its holdings follow the S&P 500 index rule-based system. It is managed in a mechanical way, linked to the actual S&P 500 index and not based on an individual manager's prediction.
- It can't underperform the market index because it *is* the market index.
- It's diversified across all market sectors.

Mutual funds have a built-in disadvantage because of their overhead. Clients pay for things like management, administrative fees, and brokerage expenses, which can range from 0.2% for an index mutual fund up to 2% for some managed funds.

The 80% of mutual fund managers that don't beat the S&P 500 still get paid, and they get paid *before* the investors regardless of how well they perform. If they manage a $100 million mutual fund and their pay is 1% of the fund, they could make $1 million a year. If their administrative fee is 2% of assets under management, then they must beat the S&P 500 by 2% just to break even. One reason that many mutual fund managers can't beat their index is that they must beat the index by the amount of their administrative fees, essentially starting in the hole.

Few professional mutual fund managers can beat the market because they try to predict the future instead of reacting to what's happening. They generally rely on their own opinions instead of following the price trends. Their incentive is to keep their job safe, not outperform their benchmark, so they usually play a defensive game. These managers will often take the safe path of investing in popular stocks and sectors.

Investors and traders that have historically beaten the market over long periods of time take a different approach from typical money managers. Mutual fund managers are almost always fully invested in stocks except for the cash they must hold for redemptions. They may rotate through sectors, but they can't go to cash during pullbacks, recessions, and bear markets. They can capture the upside of the market, but they can't protect their investors from the downside. In an upward trend, this can be a fun ride. It's not fun when the trend ends, and you lose money while the mutual fund manager still gets a payday.

The first step to beating buy and hold is to move from actively managed mutual funds to passive index mutual funds that have small management fees, or to index Exchange Traded Funds (ETF) like SPY. SPY is a ticker symbol like any other stock. By making this one change, and switching from active to passive investing, you increase your annual returns by 2% and let your money compound long-term.

Outperformance of an index happens because a stock investor or trader understands that asset prices incompletely reflect the fears and hopes of the majority. It's possible to "beat the market" over a long period by using quantified signals that create an edge through good risk/reward ratios. Market prices do react to new information or changes in the economy, but the key is to react to the trend in price and ignore predictions or opinions. The market goes through cycles of trends, extremes in prices, and it also reverts to the mean. If you can limit your downside risk and maximize the upside profits, it's possible to beat the market over the long-term.

A price filter that gets a trader or investor out before the market is down 10%, 20%, or 50% will help avoid painful corrections, bear markets, and crashes. Obviously, getting out after these things have happened is what causes underperformance and loss of capital. Likewise, investors that get out near a market top or at the beginning of a downtrend but don't know when to get back in, frequently miss the uptrend or next bull market. The solution is a simple signal that gets you out early enough to avoid big losses and gets you back in fast enough to capture large gains. One such solution is a moving average price tracking system to keep you on the right side of the market.

Summary:

- Mutual fund managers provide almost no protection from downside market risk.
- Mutual fund managers don't outperform their benchmark indexes over long periods of time, largely due to their own overhead.
- The first step in beating buy and hold investing is to not buy and hold actively managed mutual funds.
- You could increase your returns by as much as 2% a year by moving to low fee index funds or ETFs.
- The simplest way to buy into an index is to purchase an index tracking ETF or buy an index mutual fund.
- SPY is the ticker for the S&P 500 exchange traded fund.

TWO

WHY BUY AND HOLD INVESTING WORKS LONG-TERM

"The S&P 500 index] is the most historically reliable single metric of the US market over the past 140 years for both price and dividends. The early Dow 12 was too small and volatile to be a proxy for the broader US market, and the Dow of the past few decades also lacks sufficient diversification to be the best single gauge of the US equities market." – Doug Short

---

The stock market tends to go up over time, and it does eventually break old, all-time highs and move higher. This is driven by new companies and the growth of leading companies as the world economy grows. Most the profits in the stock market are made by the leadings stocks during bull markets. The long-term gains in the stock market are created by companies that go from an IPO to a Dow Jones Industrial component.

During bull markets, capital flows into equities and pushes prices up, but the stock market doesn't always go up in the short term. There may be corrections of 10%, times when prices pull back 20% in bear markets, and crashes of 50% and more during financial panics. These short-term downtrends happen even in stock indexes. Buy and hold doesn't work for most individual stocks because all companies don't trend up over time. Only those that increase their market share, keep up with technology, and maintain an edge over their competitors will win the day.

Only the best companies that grow their earnings consistently can be bought and held as an investment, and this makes a buy and hold strategy difficult for mutual funds because the fund managers must pick the winners. They essentially must know the unknowable. As we've seen in the past, seemingly sound companies have gone bankrupt and their stocks have gone to zero. This is even true for companies with household names like Circuit City, Radio Shack, Lehman Brothers, and General Motors.

Buy and hold investing is a system of betting on the long-term trend of publicly traded stocks being up over a long period. Conversely, the S&P 500 is weighted by market cap and stocks enter and leave the index based on their size. Companies that do well and grow in market capitalization enter the S&P 500, and the companies that struggle eventually fall out of the index. The most successful companies in the world that are in a price uptrend get the most weighting in the S&P 500, and the weighting drops for the less successful companies that have seen downtrends. The S&P 500 index has a survivor bias built-in, because it's designed to let winners run and drop losers out of its holdings. This makes it an effective trend following system.

Unlike mutual fund managers who may be driven by their own personal gain, the S&P 500 index is managed by a committee as a rule based system. The committee that selects the companies of the index are largely free from the pressure of quarterly returns and performance, so they can choose in a more academic, rule-based way.

Indexes are adaptive and designed to reflect the American economy. They are also diversified across different sectors. "When considering the eligibility of a new addition to the S&P 500 index, the committee assesses the company's merit using eight primary criteria: market capitalization, liquidity, domicile, public float, sector classification, financial viability, length of time publicly traded and listing exchange. The committee selects the companies in the S&P 500, so they are representative of the industries in the United States economy.

To be added to the index, a company must satisfy these liquidity-based size requirements:

- Market capitalization is greater than or equal to US$5.3 billion
- Annual dollar value traded to float-adjusted market capitalization is greater than 1.0
- Minimum monthly trading volume of 250,000 shares in each of the six months leading up to the evaluation date." – Wikipedia

I have chosen the S&P 500 index for the systems in this book rather than randomly chosen stocks, because stocks come and go but the S&P 500 index lives on with the companies that do survive. The S&P 500 index can't go bankrupt, issue false earnings, or be displaced by technology because it is diversified across all sectors and has big cap stocks; the ones that dominate their own industries.

Summary:

- The S&P 500 index is a system.
- The S&P 500 index is made up of the companies that dominate their own industries.
- The S&P 500 changes and evolves over time to represent current market leaders; it is dynamic and not stagnant.
- Indexes tend to trend higher over the long-term, while individual stocks can be winners or losers.

- Indexes can't go bankrupt thanks to diversification of companies and sectors.
- The S&P 500 is a good way to bet on the future of the U.S. economy inside a long-term mechanical trend following system.
- The S&P 500 is a safe, active investment vehicle to replace your current big cap stock buy and hold market exposure

THREE

THE EMOTIONAL FACTOR

On paper a 10% correction sounds harmless. But the reality is that losing 10% of a $250,000 401k retirement account means that you just lost $25,000. That is real, hard-earned money and the loss will be painful. One losing month isn't the end of the world, but when the next month's statement shows another 10% drop, bringing the account to $200,000---that's when bad decisions are made.

For most investors, $50,000 in two months is too much to lose, so they move their stock investments to cash the next morning. Finally, the pain and fear of loss subsides, what a relief. Unfortunately, that was the full, downside move and the market rallies back. The next month the market is back up 10%, but the investor misses and stays in cash, fearful that it's a fake move. The investor decides to wait to get back in when it pulls back to where they got out. The next following month the market is back up to even from the 20% plunge and the investor missed the move. Frustrated, they end up going back in the market at the short-term price resistance, and lose money on the next retracement because it's a range-bound year for prices.

Sadly, this story is common. Most investors lose money when they start making decisions based on their emotions rather than relying on a system they can trust. Exiting your investments when you are afraid and entering them again when you are greedy will put you on the fast track to unhappiness. The easiest way to make money is to hold stocks in bull market uptrends. The easiest way to lose money is to hold stocks through bear markets. While the stock market in general does tend to bounce back eventually, the same is not necessarily true for individual stocks.

An index is a much better choice for passive investors. Indexes are systematic and rule based in their selection of components. They pick the strongest leading stocks, they diversify across all industries, they let winners run and cut losers short, their holdings are liquid, and you can get exposure without individual transaction costs.

Summary:

- Don't discount how important your emotions are when trading. The best way to avoid making bad decisions is to keep yourself out of bad positions, especially ones that you have no control over.
- Indexes are something to consider because they are systematic and rule based, removing the emotional factor that can lead to bad decisions.
- Even though markets generally rebound at some point, individual stocks may not.

FOUR

THE DIFFERENT TIME PERIODS

"The markets are the same now as they were five to ten years ago because they keep changing – just like they did then." – Ed Seykota

---

You can't determine a trading system's effectiveness by back testing over a long period and making a quick assessment of its success. During a market peak in price, it can appear that buy and hold is the most valid approach because the market tends to come back when looking at it from the perspective of a current all-time high in price. However, during a market price bottom it will appear much less favorable.

In 2008-2009, it was possible to lose over a decade's worth of gains as a buy and hold investor, while trend followers locked in their profits before the crash. A moving average system will give you the opportunity to participate in bull markets and then exit with profits before bear markets. However, it's important to understand that your back testing time frame can cloud your judgement on a system's effectiveness, depending on the current state of the market.

You need to ask yourself the following questions:

- How did a moving average system perform during different market environments?
- How did they perform during a flat period for stocks?
- How did they perform at the market bottom?
- How did they perform at the market top?
- Did the moving average system get you out before a big market drop?
- Does the system get you back in quickly when a market starts a new uptrend in price?
- Does the market keep you in stocks during bull markets, so you receive the same gains that the buy and hold investors receive?

The purpose of these systems is to give entry signals that get you into uptrends and out before strong downtrends. They should create asymmetric risk/reward ratios where the false signals create small losses in a short period, while the signals that capture trends keep you in long-term uptrends for large gains. A moving average system should create profitability in the time frame you are trading in. A moving average system should avoid the noise of price action and only giving signals with the best potential for capturing a trend. These are the goals of a simple trend trading system.

While back testing is a good tool to see how price action patterns have acted in the past, it's not predictive of the future; think of it as a rearview mirror rather than a windshield.

Summary:

- There are different types of market environments: uptrends, downtrends, and range-bound markets.
- Moving averages should be used for the time frame you are trading in.
- Moving average systems perform differently in different type of markets.
- A moving average system should signal an entry at the beginning of a potential uptrend.
- A moving average system should signal an exit at the beginning of a potential downtrend.
- A moving average system should create big wins and small losses.
- The moving average system should be above the ordinary price action so you don't over trade.
- We want valid signals and not random noise.
- Moving average systems are reactive and not predictive.
- The past is not a prediction of the future.
- We must follow our system and let the market price action decide the result.

FIVE

MOVING AVERAGE SIGNAL #1: THE MOST POPULAR MOVING AVERAGE

"I teach an undergrad class at the University of Virginia, and I tell my students, "I'm going to save you from going to business school. Here, you're getting a $100k class, and I'm going to give it to you in two thoughts, okay? You don't need to go to business school; you've only got to remember two things. The first is, you always want to be with whatever the predominant trend is. My metric for everything I look at is the 200-day moving average of closing prices. I've seen too many things go to zero, stocks and commodities. The whole trick in investing is: "How do I keep from losing everything?" If you use the 200-day moving average rule, then you get out. You play defense, and you get out." – Paul Tudor Jones

---

*These price action back tests from www.ETFReplay.com are used by permission and are shown ONLY as examples. These back tests are unlikely to match perfectly with other platforms due to variables involved in entries, exits, and how each platform manages price data.

All back tests on ETFreplay.com assume that trades are executed on the close, never the open. These were my settings for this back test and are subject to the variables that this platform uses compared to other testing software. Dividends are included in the back tests.

You will enter this system the first time that price crosses back up over the 200-day SMA. The following back tests are based on the first cross. The back test will wait until ETF crosses above the moving average before making the first buy. This system waits for a better risk/reward ratio to enter at a break back over the 200-day SMA. For this system, you must wait for an initial monthly crossover and close over the 200-day SMA rather than entering and taking a position on the first day of trading, because the results will be skewed with an initial bad risk/reward entry at elevated levels.

This system's signals are taken at month end rather than on the day of the actual cross. This is a slow, long-term system that looks to enter or exit at the end of the last day of the month, based on whether price has crossed over or under the 200-day SMA. This system has a maximum potential of twelve signals in one year.

This was the 200-day simple moving average used:

- Moving Average is based on the total return data series that includes dividends and distributions.
- The simple moving average is the average (arithmetic mean) of the specified number of data points.
- The 200-day moving average is the average of 200 daily total return values

Because the first system is taking a signal only once per month rather than daily, it means accepting more risk. However, studying this system will help you decide if you would rather take on more risk, or be subjected to more frequent false signals, as with the other systems in this book.

Let's look at how this moving average system would do if traded during the 21st century of bull markets, bear markets, sideways markets, and crashes:

- From January 3, 2000 to December 9, 2016: $SPY buy and hold had a gain of 125.2% with a maximum drawdown of -55.2% during the same period for a 200-day SMA end of month system.
- $SPY using the 200-day SMA as an end of month sell/buy indicator from January 3, 2000 to December 9, 2016: The 200-day SMA end of month system returned 317.7% and had a maximum drawdown of 17.3%. This system almost tripled returns and cut the drawdown by over two-thirds.

How did this moving average system do during a decade long sideways market?

- From March 24, 2000 to December 30, 2011: $SPY buy and hold had a gain of 7% with a maximum drawdown of -55.2% during the same period for a 200-day SMA end of month system.
- $SPY using the 200-day SMA as an end of month sell/buy indicator from March 24, 2000 to December 30, 2011: The 200-day SMA end of month system returned 112.6% and had maximum drawdown of 17.3%.

How would this moving average system do if traded from the stock market peak to the stock market bottom?

Chart courtesy of stockcharts.com

- From October 11, 2007 to March 9, 2009: $SPY buy and hold had a loss of -52.8% with a maximum drawdown of -55.2% during the same period for a 200-day SMA system.
- For $SPY using the 200-day SMA as an end of month sell/buy indicator from October 11, 2007 to March 9, 2009: The 200-day SMA system lost -1.1% and had a maximum drawdown of -4.6%, avoiding big losses and cutting the drawdown by over 90%.

This is a very simple trend trading system that even casual investors can use because you only need to worry about it on the last day of the month, with signals primarily being taken at the beginning of a bull market and the beginning of a potential bear market. This system generally keeps you on the right side of the long-term trend; long during bull markets and in cash during downtrends.

This system will filter out the false signals on end of day and end of week as it is on a longer time frame. This system looks for the long-term uptrend of the stock market and to avoid the bear market cycles until price trend has reversed.

Using this system, your signals will be taken on the last day of the month. If price crosses over the 200-day SMA inside the month and closes over it on the last day of the month, you will enter and go long. If the price crosses under the 200-day SMA inside the month and then closes under the 200-day SMA, you will go to cash. You will do this twelve times a year.

SIX

MOVING AVERAGE SIGNAL #2: AVOID NOISE

These were my settings for this back test and are subject to the variables that this platform uses compared to other testing software. Dividends are included in the back tests.

You will enter this system on the first day that price crosses back up over the 250-day SMA at the end of that trading day. The following back tests are based on the first cross. The back test will wait until the ETF crosses above the moving average before making the first buy. This system waits for a better risk/reward ratio to enter at a break back over the 250-day SMA. You should wait to enter, or the results will be skewed with an initial bad risk/reward entry at elevated levels. In most cases, the daily price crossover will likely be a pullback in the market and price will already be above the 250-day SMA, except during corrections and bear markets.

This system's signals are taken at the end of the day, the same day of the cross. This is the daily chart time frame, and a long-term system that looks to enter or exit at the end of the day based on whether price is over or under the 250-day SMA. It only gives a signal at that cross, and the system may go weeks or months without a signal. You will be in cash when price is below the 250-day and long when price is above the 250-day SMA. This system will keep you long through bull markets, will likely take you to cash as a market starts to go into a correction, and will help you avoid the worst of bear markets and crashes.

This was the 250-day simple moving average used:

- This 250-day moving average of prices is based on the total return data series that includes dividends and distributions.
- The simple moving average is the average (arithmetic mean) of the specified number of data points.
- The 250-day moving average is the average of 250 daily total return values

This system means accepting more risk of giving back capital gains during a bull market by waiting until the 250-day SMA is crossed instead of just the 200-day SMA. However, this second option helps to avoid the noise of false moves through the 200-day moving average in a bull market.

This system gets you out faster than the month end system and helps you avoid sharp monthly moves. It will also get you back in quicker if the market rallies strong on the daily chart versus a monthly system. Unlike the first system, this one requires you to be more active, watching to see if price is close to the 250-day moving average for several days in row.

The main drawback of this second system is that the signals can move back and forth, and you can lose money when price is near the 250-day SMA and the price range is volatile and causes false signals.

How would this system do if traded during the 21st century of bull markets, bear markets, sideways markets, and crashes?

- From January 3, 2000 to December 9, 2016: $SPY buy and hold had a gain of 127.4% with a maximum

drawdown of -55.2% during the same period as the
signals for a 250-day SMA end of day system.
- $SPY using the 250-day SMA as an end of day sell/buy
  indicator from January 3, 2000 to December 9, 2016:
  The 250-day SMA end of day system returned 128% and
  had maximum drawdown of 23.1%. This system can
  duplicate the returns of buy and hold with less than half
  the drawdown.

How did this moving average system do during a decade long
sideways market?

- From March 24, 2000 to December 30, 2011: $SPY buy
  and hold had a gain of 10.3% with a maximum
  drawdown of -55.2% during the same period as the
  signals for a 250-day SMA end of day system.
- $SPY using the 250-day SMA as an end of day sell/buy
  indicator from March 24, 2000 to December 30, 2011:
  The 250-day SMA end of day system returned 31.8%
  and had maximum drawdown of 23.1%. This system
  tripled buy and hold returns and cut drawdowns in half,
  but it needs a long-term uptrend to make good returns.

How would this moving average system do if traded from the
stock market peak to the stock market bottom?

Chart Courtesy of StockCharts.com

- From October 11, 2007 to March 9, 2009: $SPY buy and hold had a loss of -52.7% with a maximum drawdown of -55.2%.
- $SPY using the 250-day SMA as an end of day sell/buy indicator from October 11, 2007 to March 9, 2009: The 250-day SMA system lost -3.8% with a maximum drawdown of -5.3%. This system cut the drawdown by almost 90%.

SEVEN

MOVING AVERAGE SIGNAL #3: THE GOLDEN AND DEATH CROSSES

These were my settings for this back test and are subject to the variables that this platform uses compared to other testing software. Dividends are included in the back tests.

You will enter this system on the first day that the 50-day SMA crosses back over the 200-day SMA. The following back tests are based on the first cross. The back test will wait until the ETF crosses above the moving average before making the first buy. This system waits for a better trend signal to enter after a 50-day/200-day SMA crossover. This is not a system to enter immediately as the results will be skewed with an initial bad risk/reward entry at elevated levels if the moving averages have already crossed.

 This system's signals are taken at the end of the day on the day of moving average crossover. This is the daily chart time frame and it is a long-term system. It only looks to enter or exit at the end of the day based on whether the 50-day SMA is over or under the 200-day SMA. It only gives a signal at this crossover, and this system may go weeks or months with no entry or exit signals. You will be in cash when the 50-day SMA is below the 200-day SMA and long when the 50-day SMA is above the 200-day SMA.

This is a moving average crossover system which means that you are trading one moving average crossing another moving average instead of price crossing a moving average. This system will keep you long through strong bull markets, will likely take you to cash as a market starts to trend downward, and will help you avoid large pull-backs, bear markets, and crashes.

This is the moving average crossover system that was used:

- 50-day simple moving average and the 200-day simple moving average. This 50-day and 200-day moving averages of prices is based on the total return data series that includes dividends and distributions.
- The simple moving average is the average (arithmetic mean) of the specified number of data points.
- The 50-day moving average is the average of 50 daily total return values.
- The 200-day moving average is the average of 200 daily total return values.

This system only takes a signal when the 50-day SMA moves through the 200-day SMA on the daily time frame. This system attempts to balance the risk of giving back capital gains during a bull market, and staying long when an uptrend is confirmed. However, this third option helps with faster signals than waiting for price to move back to the 200-day or 250-day SMAs.

This system usually gets you out slower than the 250-day SMA or the 200-day end of month system and helps you avoid any false downward moves. This system will also get you back in slower to avoid a lot of false moves due to volatility if the market rallies strong on the daily chart. The 50-day and 200-day SMA are you signal lines, and you will find this to be a less active system with fewer signals.

How would this moving average system do if traded during the 21st century of bull markets, bear markets, sideways markets, and crashes?

- From January 3, 2000 to December 9, 2016: $SPY buy and hold had a gain of +167.1% with a maximum drawdown of -55.2% during the same period as the first signal generated for the 50-day/200-day SMA end of day system test.
- $SPY using the 50-day SMA crossover of the 200-day SMA as an end of day buy signal, and the 50-day SMA crossing under the 200-day SMA as an end of day sell signal to go to cash from
- January 3, 2000 to December 9, 2016: The 50-day/200-day SMA crossover end of day system returned +204.9% and had maximum drawdown of -19.2%.

How did this moving average system do during a decade long sideways market?

- From March 24, 2000 to December 30, 2011: $SPY buy and hold had a gain of 34.3% with a maximum drawdown of -55.2% during the same period as the signals for a 50-day SMA/200-day SMA end of day system.
- $SPY using the 50-day SMA/ 200-day SMA crossover system as an end of day sell/buy indicator from March 24, 2000 to December 30, 2011: The 50-day SMA/200-day SMA end of day system returned 90.8% and had a maximum drawdown of 17.3%. This system beat buy and hold returns and decreased drawdown by two-thirds.

How would this moving average system do if traded from the stock market peak to the stock market bottom?

- From October 11, 2007 to March 9, 2009: $SPY buy and hold had a loss of -52.7% with a maximum drawdown of -55.2%

Chart Courtesy of StockCharts.com

- From October 11, 2007 to March 9, 2009 there was no new crossover signal to enter long during this entire cycle. The system signaled to stay in cash if you weren't already long from a previous entry signal. If you were in $SPY before this time frame, it would have signaled you to go to cash by January of 2008 to avoid the crash after the 50-day crossed under the 200-day.

EIGHT

MOVING AVERAGE SIGNAL #4: A POPULAR CROSSOVER SYSTEM

*These were my settings for this back test and are subject to the variables that this platform uses compared to other testing software. Dividends are included in the back tests.

You will enter this system on the first day that the 20-day SMA crosses back over the 200-day SMA. The following back tests are based on the first cross. The back test will wait until the ETF crosses above the moving average before making the first buy. This system waits for a trend signal to enter after a 20-day/200-day SMA crossover. This is not a system to enter immediately because the results will be skewed with an initial bad risk/reward entry at elevated levels if the moving averages have already crossed.

This system's signals are taken at the end of the day on the day of the moving average crossover. This is a daily chart time frame and it's a long-term system. It only looks to enter or exit at the end of the day based on whether the 20-day SMA is over or under the 200-day SMA. It only gives a signal at this crossover, and you can wait weeks or months for a signal. You will be in cash when the 20-day SMA is below the 200-day SMA and long when the 20-day SMA is above the 200-day SMA.

This is a moving average crossover system which means that you are trading one moving average crossing another moving average instead of price crossing a moving average. This system will keep you long through strong bull markets, will most likely take you to cash at the first sign a market starts to trend downward, and help you avoid pullbacks, bear markets, and crashes.

This is the moving average crossover system that was used:

- This system uses the 20-day simple moving average and the 200-day moving average. The 20-day and 200-day moving averages of prices is based on the total return data series, which includes dividends and distributions.
- The simple moving average is the average (arithmetic mean) of the specified number of data points.
- The 20-day moving average is the average of 20 daily total return values.
- The 200-day moving average is the average of 200 daily total return values.

This system takes a signal only when the 20-day SMA moves through the 200-day SMA on the daily time frame. This system attempts to balance the risk of giving back capital gains during a fast pullback in a bull market, with staying long when an uptrend is quickly confirmed. This system has faster signals than the previous three moving average systems.

This system gets you back in very quickly if the market rallies strong on the daily chart. And it could get you long closer to the bottom of bear markets depending on the speed of an early rally. The 20-day/200-day crossover system delays your entry from when price crosses over the 200-day or 250-day SMA and helps avoid false signals and volatility.

You must watch this system more closely than the other systems to see if a 20-day/ 200-day moving average cross is about to happen. This could be a less choppy than the first two systems, and you'll get faster signals than the last example.

How would this moving average system do if traded during the 21st century of bull markets, bear markets, sideways markets, and crashes?

- From January 3, 2000 to December 9, 2016: $SPY buy and hold had a gain of +161.6% with a maximum drawdown of -55.2% during the same period as the first signal generated for the 20-day/200-day SMA end of day system test.
- $SPY using the 20-day SMA crossover of the 200-day SMA as an end of day buy signal, and the 20-day SMA crossing under the 200-day SMA as a sell signal to go to cash from January 3, 2000 to December 9, 2016: The 20-day/200-day SMA crossover end of day system returned +193% and had maximum drawdown of -17.3%.

How did this moving average system do during a decade long sideways market?

- From March 24, 2000 to December 30, 2011: $SPY buy and hold had a gain of +31.5% with a maximum drawdown of -55.2% during the same period as the signals for a 20-day SMA/200-day SMA end of day system.
- $SPY using the 20-day SMA/ 200-day SMA crossover system as an end of day sell/buy indicator from March 24, 2000 to December 30, 2011: The 20-day SMA/200-day SMA end of day system returned +67.9% and had a maximum drawdown of -17.3%. This system doubled buy and hold returns and decreased drawdown by two-thirds.

Chart Courtesy of StockCharts.com

How would this moving average system do if you traded it from the stock market peak to the stock market bottom?

- From October 11, 2007 to March 9, 2009 there was no new crossover signal to enter long during this entire cycle. The system stayed in cash if you were not already long from a previous entry signal. If you were in $SPY before this time frame, it would have signaled you to go to cash by December of 2008 and avoid the crash after the 20-day crossed under the 200-day.

NINE

MOVING AVERAGE SIGNAL #5: BASIC TREND FOLLOWING

Here are the variables that this platform uses to help understand any variance against other back testing sites or software. These were my settings. Dividends are included in the back tests.

You will enter this system on the first day that the 50-day SMA crosses back over the 100-day SMA. The following back tests are based on the first cross. The back test will wait until the ETF crosses above the moving average before making the first buy. This system waits for a better trend signal to enter after a 50-day/100-day SMA crossover. This is not a system to enter immediately, because the results will be skewed with an initial bad risk/reward entry at elevated levels if the moving averages have already crossed.

This system's signals are taken at the end of the day on the day of the moving average crossover. This is the daily chart time frame, and it is a long-term system that only looks to enter or exit at the end of the day based on whether the 50-day SMA is over or under the 100-day SMA. It only gives a signal at this crossover, and this system can go weeks or months with no entry or exit signals. You will be in cash when the 50-day SMA is below the 100-day SMA and long when the 50-day SMA is above the 100-day SMA.

This is a moving average crossover system which means that you are trading one moving average crossing another moving average instead of price crossing a moving average. This system will keep you long through strong bull markets, will most likely take you to cash as a market starts to trend downward, and help you avoid large pullbacks, bear markets, and crashes.

This is the moving average crossover system that was used:

- This system uses the 50-day simple moving average and the 100-day moving average.
- The 50-day and 100-day moving averages of price is based on the total return data series that includes dividends and distributions.
- The simple moving average is the average (arithmetic mean) of the specified number of data points.
- The 50-day moving average is the average of 50 daily total return values.
- The 100-day moving average is the average of 100 daily total return values.

This system takes a signal only when the 50-day SMA moves through the 100-day SMA on the daily time frame. This system attempts to balance the risk of giving back capital gains during a bull market with staying long when an uptrend is confirmed. This option improves performance by reducing the time frame of the long-term moving average signal.

This system generally gets you out faster than the 50-day/ 200-day cross, 250-day SMA, or the 200-day end of month system. It will also get you back in quicker if the market rallies strong on the daily chart versus the 50-day/ 200-day crossover, 250-day, or a monthly system. This can be a more active system to use because you must watch for the 50-day/ 100-day moving average cross.

How would this moving average system do if you traded it during the 21st century of bull markets, bear markets, sideways markets, and crashes?

- From January 3, 2000 to December 9, 2016: $SPY buy and hold had a gain of +103.9% with a maximum drawdown of -55.2% during the same period as the first signal generated for the 50-day/100-day SMA end of day system test.
- $SPY using the 50-day SMA crossover of the 100-day SMA as an end of day buy signal, and the 50-day SMA crossing under the 100-day SMA as a sell signal to go to cash from January 3, 2000 to December 9, 2016: The 50-day/100-day SMA crossover end of day system returned +127.2% and had maximum drawdown of -19.4%.

How did this moving average system do during a decade long sideways market?

- From March 24, 2000 to December 30, 2011: $SPY buy and hold had a gain of +2.5% with a maximum drawdown of -55.2% during the same period as the initial signal for a 50-day SMA/100-day SMA end of day system.
- $SPY using the 50-day SMA/ 100-day SMA crossover system as an end of day sell/buy indicator from March 24, 2000 to December 30, 2011: The 50-day SMA/100-day SMA end of day system returned +54.1% and had a maximum drawdown of -19.4%. This system beat buy and hold returns during the time of its signals and decreased drawdown by over half during the flat market.

How would this moving average system do if you traded it from the stock market peak to the stock market bottom?

Chart Courtesy of StockCharts.com

- From October 11, 2007 to March 9, 2009: during the same period of this signal entry and exit, $SPY buy and hold had a loss of -53.7% with a maximum drawdown of -55.2%.
- $SPY using the 50-day SMA crossing over the 100-day SMA as an end of day buy indicator, and a 50-day SMA crossing back under the 100-day SMA as an end of day sell signal from October 11, 2007 to March 9, 2009: The 50/100-day SMA crossover system lost -12.9% and had maximum drawdown of -16.7%.

CONCLUSION

These moving average systems are not meant to be the Holy Grail of investing. These systems are basic examples of the principles of trend following systems that are on a time frame like buy and hold, and require few actions until the signal for entry or exit is near. This permits a trend trader to have a quantified system to enter at the beginning of a potential trend, let a winning trade go as far as possible, and exit to lock in profits before a bear market, correction, or market crash.

These systems use the principles of asymmetric risk/reward by using moving averages on a time frame that keeps you fully invested for as long as possible during strong bull markets, rallies, and uptrends so you can stockpile profits. They take you back to cash at the first sign of danger, so you have smaller losses.

The systems in this book could lead to losses if the market is volatile. You could be stopped out and be forced to re-enter several times. An overbought market means that you could wait for months before a pullback and a crossover entry is given. Patience and discipline are the keys to making these systems work for you.

A back test is not predictive, and it's not perfect. It is a historical sample of how price action behaved in the past. We can't predict the future, so it's important to employ proper risk management, a valid trading system, and the discipline to choose and follow a methodology that fits our personality. Remember that back tests are just one of the tools in your toolbox.

Things to remember:

- They are on long enough time frames to avoid getting excessive entry and exit signals. Short time frames will deliver too many signals and impair your ability to capitalize on trends.
- The moving averages in this book give you enough room to capture the long-term uptrend but are generally fast enough to get you out before things take a turn for the worse.
- If an exit signal is false and the market rallies, these moving average systems are fast enough on a time frame that will get you back in quickly, so you can catch upward trends.
- These systems get you in on the first cross signal, so you enter only with a good risk/reward at the first entry signal.
- These systems will only work if they are followed with discipline over the long-term. You can adjust them, but the new parameters must to be back tested for validity through multiple market environments.
- The moving average systems in this book have been tested over a 16-year period, capturing the beginning and end of bull markets, through bear markets, and market crashes. They are a good sample of how they perform during different market environments.
- Back tests are not predictions of the future or guarantees

of future performance. The odds are that patterns repeat themselves, because people's emotional reactions repeat over time to create trends.

- We choose our system, position size, and markets to trade, the market will choose our returns.

Happy Trading!

Follow Steve at NewTraderU.com or on Twitter at @sjosephburns.

ABOUT THE DATA

A special thank you to ETFReplay.com and Stockcharts.com for the use of their data and charts included in this book. They are invaluable resources and we are appreciative of their willingness to help all of us become better investors and traders.

- 17 high quality videos covering the best way to enter and exit your trades for a profit
- Step-by-step examples
- More than 30 annotated charts

Join Price Action Trading 101 today!

Moving Averages 101– Everything you need to know to harness the power of Moving Averages and take your trading to the next level!
In this Moving Averages 101 eCourse, you'll get:

- 11 professional videos that will teach you how to use moving averages in your trading strategy.
- Specific article recommendations provided for every lesson so you can continue your trading education.
- More than 45 detailed charts with step-by-step explanations to help you understand not only the how, but the why.

Join Moving Averages 101 today!

Options 101 –
This 19-part video course is packed with information about Options, and how they can help you up your trading game. It includes real trading examples, many visuals, and an Options Play Strategy Guide that you won't find anywhere else.
In the Options 101 eCourse, you'll get:

- 19 high quality videos covering how and why to trade
- Step-by-step trading examples
- Many annotated charts

Join Options 101 today!

Did you enjoy this eBook?

Please consider writing a review.

Listen to many of our titles on Audible!

Read more of our bestselling titles available *exclusively* on Amazon:

Moving Averages 101
So You Want to be a Trader
New Trader 101
Moving Averages 101
Buy Signals and Sell Signals
Trading Habits
Investing Habits
Calm Trader